ISBN: 978-1-9991103-0-7

DEDICATION

To everyone who desires to live a life of purpose to make the world a better place than they met it.

ACKNOWLEDGEMENT

I want to thank my dear parents, Bar and Mrs. Peter Igietsemhe Momodu for the guidance and personal sacrifices they made to help me live a life of purpose.

I also thank my brothers, Ogie, Kpemi and Igemokhai and all my friends for their immense support through the writing of this book.

I also appreciate the time and efforts of the team at Brilliant Writers Academy.

God bless you all.

TABLE OF CONTENTS

PREFACE

Since the publishing of my book *Success Basics*, the most common question I've received from people is about understanding their life purpose. I believe this question is increasingly more important because people find out after several years that many things they have done in life did not really matter and have not found fulfilment in doing them. In this book you'll find the lessons to guide you through the discovery of your purpose and walking towards a life of fulfilment.

As our society evolves with new challenges every day, it is becoming clearer that a life of purpose is the best way to live. In America for example, it was reported[1] that over a million American lives have been lost due to "deaths of despair" caused by suicide and other psychological issues, particularly amongst the working class. As the world tries to address this current menace that could keep increasing; I believe the main issue we must address now is not only about the alarming number of people who die after they lose hope but a likely larger number of people currently living with a loss of hope.

If you live a life of purpose, it brings a sense of meaning to everything you do irrespective of challenges or contradictions. A sense of meaning guarantees a sense of hope that helps you live life with passion, joy and enthusiasm looking forward to a glorious future.

The question of purpose is not an easy question with a blanket answer for everyone. The answer is very personal and so I have titled the book, "Why am I here?" and not "Why are we here?". It is a guide for you specifically with exercises after every chapter for you to coach yourself. To get the most from this book, I encourage you to complete each exercise before going to the next chapter. Take your time to complete them in a place of serenity where you can think clearly and be as honest as possible. I encourage you to also be as open as possible to learn and make the changes needed for maximum results. The degree of clarity and inspired actions you'd get from each exercise depends on the level of honesty and openness you put into them. You can also get an accountability partner to help you keep this commitment to honesty and doing the exercises.

I also observed in writing this book that you would likely get some inspiration as you read along and reflect on your story. Do not wait till the end of the chapters, get a pen and journal and write down your thoughts clearly. This would help you gain more clarity when you answer the questions.

Just a little word here to appeal to reader sentiments, I have used *man* here to refer to both the male and female man[2].

COMMITMENT

I commit to studying this book and answering all the exercises with honesty.

_____   _____

Your name   *Signature*

_____   _____

Accountability partner   *Signature*

_____

Date.

Enjoy this voyage of discovery!

CHAPTER ONE

INTRODUCTION

"Life is a question and how we live it is our answer"
– Gary Keller

Claudia shared an emotional story with me recently as I wrote this book. At about fourth year in medical school, she was diagnosed of a congenital heart disease that required a surgery. Amid the pain and shock, she underwent surgery and was lucky to scale through alive. During that period of recovery, she realized, what if I died? What is the struggle in life about? What would I have lived for?

Moments of reflection made her realize she had gotten a second chance at life and the reality hit home that you only get a chance to live once. It became clear to her that she had accepted to be a doctor because of her parents, respect in the society and did not feel passionate about going through all the hurdles of medical certifications.

Her passion for business was stronger in her heart and she knew she preferred an education in that line. She was starting to weigh her options to get an MBA when we discussed.

Your story may not be exactly like Claudia's, you may not have experienced the pain of standing at the edge of life but many times you would have asked similar questions she asked about the purpose of life. The question of purpose is still one of the most important questions that plague people today. Many ask themselves in private, why am I here? Why am I doing this? And the truth remains that until you answer the question of purpose, you have not known the true essence of life. Until you find the true essence of your being, life would be utterly meaningless and remain a struggle. The wealthiest king that ever lived who had the testimony of giving himself anything his body asked for had this testimony that a life without purpose is simply vanity upon vanity[3].

Life is a jungle of hustles and bustles with no clear meaning except there is a good reason for the ride. Purpose gives you clarity and until you get clear about the kind of life you want, you would not be clear about the path to get there. Before I share with you what purpose is, I like to clear some misconceptions many people have about the question of purpose. Let's look at what purpose is not before looking at what purpose is.

WHAT PURPOSE IS NOT

In a coaching session with a young lady, she complained of not finding anything easy to do that could be a clue to her purpose. She was good in writing, speaking and graphic designing but claimed to find them difficult. She was interested in finding out her purpose where she would do things with ease. This is just one of the many misconceptions that people have about purpose.

Purpose does not mean easy

Today everyone is seeking for ways to make things easier. There is an increasing reference to building things around your comfort zone or enlarging your comfort zone. Like the young lady, I've always loved writing too. In completing my first book, *Success Basics*, there were nights I had to sleep late to edit my book. I had to invest money in getting a proper book cover design, professional editing and interior design. Sacrificing my time, money and energy wasn't easy but it was worth it because this was in alignment with my purpose. My focus on impacting lives kept me going and not a desire to find things easy. Purpose does not mean easy, it only means you committed to walk in a path because you find joy and fulfillment in doing it. I have not written this book to help you find the easiest way to live life but rather the most fulfilling path to follow. It is true that we all have natural abilities to help us in fulfilling purpose but these natural abilities alone would not fulfill your purpose. In the book,

Talent is never enough, John Maxwell rightly shares additional values needed to increase the effectiveness of our talents and one of them is hard work. Purpose is not a short-cut for instant gratification, and sometimes people get discouraged in life because they have developed an inner belief system that life was made to be easy. Life could be easy but not in the sense of reducing your strengths and ability.

Purpose does not mean money

You would be wrong if you are seeking to fulfil your purpose because you want to make money. There are many things you could do to make money that are not necessarily your purpose. Money opportunities are there to help you fund your purpose. Your purpose is the main goal while money opportunities are a means to an end. You could miss a lot of opportunities if you allow money to be the driver for seeking purpose.

> **Purpose is first a service to humanity and not a money-making venture.**

If purpose was about money, Moses would prefer to live in Pharaoh's palace rather than to be in the wilderness[5]. In contemporary times, the story of Mother Teresa still inspires so many today. A catholic Nun who left the comfort of the convent to live with and help the poorest poor in India.

You could be a real estate investor, you could get a job doing XYZ, or start a business that provides value in the market place. Making money through any of these is not necessarily your purpose but it could generate a lot of income to help fund your purpose. Your purpose could also bring value to the market place and generate much income but purpose is first a service to humanity and not a money-making venture.

Purpose does not mean wants

Growing up in a humble family, I was eager to make enough money to help my family and people around me. So as a young chap, I started seeking for the best career with the highest earnings. At first, I chose farming, thinking agriculture may be a good source of income but I later chose to be an Accountant because we had a neighbor who worked as one and they were financially set. Then one day I was watching a movie and saw an Accountant get totally wrecked for signing a wrong check. That got to me and I decided to seek for another career. I later settled for Petroleum Engineering because oil and gas workers were the top earners in Nigeria then. Well, the University of Benin eventually offered me admission in Production Engineering and thank God I was good in mathematics; who knows how miserable studying a course I chose only for money would have been. Purpose does not mean what you want to be but rather who you need to be and who God created you to be. if you want to know why you are here on earth, you need to open your heart to find out what God wants you to be.

Purpose is not only for the young

A forty-one-year-old friend contacted me complaining about how badly her life had turned out. She had a child out of wedlock and it seemed she wasn't enjoying her marriage. What struck me in the story though was her passion for women and her desire to help women going through tough times in marriage. This has been a desire for a long time but now she feels too old to start it. I was quick to correct that notion and point to others who fulfilled purpose at a much later age. Abraham could have thought God had abandoned him at seventy-five[6]. What purpose could there be that an old man would not have seen already at seventy-five years old? But then at that old age, God showed up and made him a Father of many nations. Do not allow your age limit your dream. As long as there is life, there is a purpose to be fulfilled.

Purpose does not mean lone-ranger

Uniqueness of purpose does not translate to you being a lone ranger. This is a problem especially for introverts, the desire to complete projects with all our strength and might. I know this because I'm an introvert. We have a very high tendency to be a lone-ranger without seeking for help. You have a purpose to fulfill does not mean you are the only one who would fulfill that purpose. We must learn to create room for others and seek help from others connected to fulfilling that purpose. God created man to be interdependent, we see this in Gen. 2:15 where God said, it is not good for man to be alone.

Anyone who God sent to fulfill purpose in the Bible, did not do so on their own, Moses had Aaron, Nehemiah had Ezra, Joseph had the chief baker and even Jesus had twelve disciples. Of course, not everyone has to accept your purpose, it is possible you are the first person to find a need and desire to meet it but along the journey to fulfilment, learn to connect with people God would send your way. It can have a multiplying effect on your purpose.

WHAT IS PURPOSE?

Knowing fully well what purpose is not, I believe you are curious to identify what purpose really means. Let us examine the creation of the smartphones to understand the true meaning of purpose. The smartphone is probably the most popular accessory we carry around today. You are probably reading this book on your smart phone. Why are phones available today? Martin Rogers was the first to invent wireless communication. He saw a need because snail mail was taking several days and the logistic was becoming more difficult. Imagine having to send "Hello" to your loved one and wait for a week to get "Hi" in reply. This was the case with communication back in the days.

The purpose of a thing is in the heart of its creator.

With determination in his heart and a clear purpose of easing communications between individuals, Martin went to his lab and came up with the first means of wireless communication. The phone was created eventually with a clear purpose in the mind of the creator Martin and a clear question to answer. There is a clear purpose for everything made and the purpose of a thing is in the heart of its creator. The creation is useless apart from being used in alignment with its purpose. Imagine using your phone to eat a hot bowl of rice? Awkward! Because it wasn't made with that purpose in mind.

God is the creator of man and He had a purpose in mind for creating man. We see the general purpose of God for creating man in Gen. 1:28 and we see an example of a specific purpose of God for creating man when He spoke to Prophet Jeremiah in Jer. 1:5. The purpose of a thing is not an afterthought; the purpose is built into the creation. No matter who you are, where you are or what you may be doing, God has a purpose for your life. This book is written to help you discover that specific purpose of God for your life.

"Then God blessed them, and God said to them, "Be fruitful and multiply; fill the earth and subdue it; have dominion over the fish of the sea, over the birds of the air, and over every living thing that moves on the earth.'" – Gen. 1:28

"Before I formed you in the womb, I knew you; Before you were born, I sanctified you; I ordained you a prophet to the nations." – Jer. 1:5

Definitions of purpose

Purpose is the reason God created you

Purpose is the reason for being

Purpose is the life question your life answers

Purpose is the key to living a fulfilled life.

Purpose is the need of humanity your life meets.

Purpose is the legacy your life would leave on earth.

Purpose is God's plan for your life.

Purpose is the goal of your life.

Purpose is the ultimate use of all your abilities for the service of humanity.

Purpose is making the world better than you met it.

Purpose is the value your life adds.

Purpose is a responsibility you owe your generation.

During my undergrad studies, in a hall of over five hundred students, the vice-chancellor asked students who were admitted to courses they didn't apply for to raise their hands. Close to eighty percent in the hall that day raised their hands. I was dazed. It is either they have been put in the right course by divine providence or they have been put on a wrong path. This is not only in schools though, many are working in jobs not in alignment with their purpose and all they do is go to work, earn an income, sleep, wake and get sad without any recourse to living their life purpose. Others are even in relationships and locations in total misalignment from divine purpose. You must understand that success without fulfilment is the ultimate failure in life. Fulfilment can only come when we walk in alignment with our purpose.

People have resorted to different things to fill the vacuum of purpose fulfillment. If you are stuck in drug addiction, an immoral life, alcoholism or wrong relationships, it is very certain you are not walking in alignment with your life's purpose. The end of this is only misery, regrets and frustration. A life of purpose is not automatic or by chance, it takes careful dedication and an intentional drive to discover your purpose and grow in alignment with it for its eventual fulfilment. The purpose triangle below explains the different stages for purpose fulfilment. You will learn more details on what to do at each of these stages in the upcoming chapters.

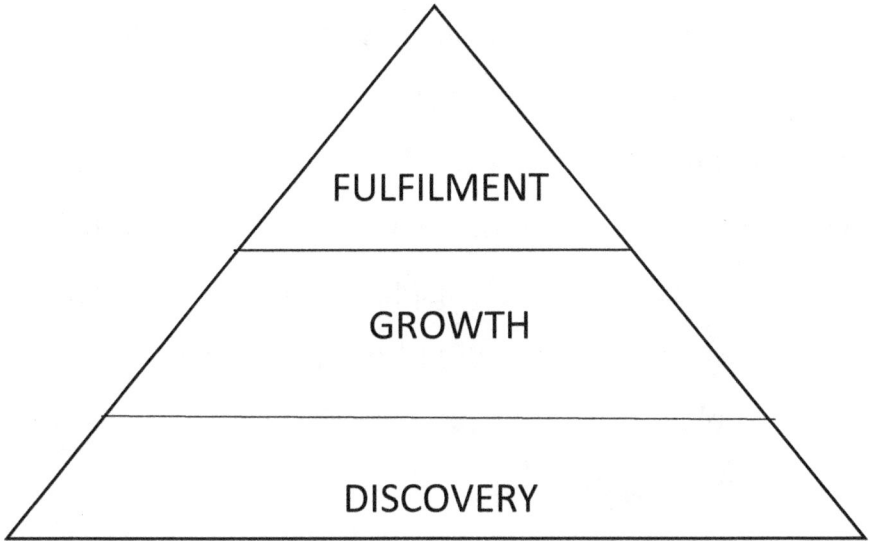

Fig. 1: Purpose triangle

Each level of the purpose triangle is similar to the different phases of life. Understanding the different phases of life would help you maximize your full potentials for maximum impact.

LIFE'S PHASES

You go through life in phases. I have divided these phases into three here. The *searching phase, growth phase, execution phase.* It is important to understand these phases for a clearer and better purpose journey. The searching phase is the phase for answering life questions. You must have seen this manifest in children. They are always curious about life. They ask questions about where we all come from, what they'd become in life or where God is. The searching phase opens you up to learn new ideas for your growth in life. After this phase is the growth phase where you start learning various life lessons through experience.

You may start relationships that end up not working out, business ideas could fail or succeed and you may start a course or job you love or end up not loving. This is the phase you must be patient with yourself as you go through life lessons and be totally immersed in it to acquire the knowledge and experience required for your execution phase. The growth phase can be seen as an exploratory phase. You more flexible to explore new ideas that help your growth.

In the execution phase you start implementing lessons from your growth phase. If you learnt relationship lessons properly, it can help you be a better spouse. Your business lessons in your growth phase can help you start a bigger and better business in your execution phase. The execution phase is an exploitation phase where you exploit the lessons that worked well in your growth phase. In this phase you would also find the appropriate mediums to deplore your purpose to help humanity. If you are wondering why things may not be working in your life as fast as you thought, you may still be at your growth phase learning lessons in preparation for your execution phase. I'd share with you a story that helped me understand life's phases better.

After many trips along the Lagos-Benin express road in Nigeria during my undergraduate days, I noticed an ugly structure being built by the road side. I always wondered what this ugly structure could be. After some time, on completion, it turned out to be a beautiful bank edifice. This taught me that life may not be pretty at some stage, but it turns out beautiful when we are patient for everything to come together.

The searching phase is like the building foundation where you get some level of clarity to your purpose amongst other life questions. The growth phase is the phase for building on the foundation and things may look ugly at this phase but it gets beautiful when you start completions in the execution phase. The beauty of an ongoing construction may not be seen by passers-by but the original plan already has the beauty of the household in the hands of the architect. This is also true for a life of purpose. God has a purpose for your life and that purpose is made manifest through the different phases of life he takes you through.

The following coaching session would help you gain clarity on your current phase in your purpose journey.

COACHING SESSION

1. What does purpose mean to you?

2. On a scale on 1 to 10, 1 being lowest and 10 highest, rate how well you believe you are made for more.

3. In what phase of life do you think you are?

There are some people who do not believe in the value they carry. They do not believe God created them for a purpose and this is largely due to a negative self-image. In the next chapter you'd have a self-image map coaching session and learn the different components of a positive self-image.

CHAPTER TWO

FIRST THINGS FIRST

"Popularity is when other people like you, happiness is when you like yourself"
-Mike Murdock

Daniel contacted me recently that he was seriously eager to know his purpose. At eighteen, I believe Daniel should have some clue on where his life leads but he claimed to be blank about this. I asked several questions about his passion, natural abilities and dreams. He feigned ignorance and claimed he doesn't believe he is worth anything as his friends usually say. I got to know where the real problem was after he said this. He had a wrong self-image and this made nothing else matter. He had a negative self-image from what his friends had said about him. This is the most important part of a life of purpose. You must first believe in yourself before you can believe in your purpose. People may not support your dreams or see the purpose you have in you, the most important person who must believe in you is you.

Your self-image is your inner picture of your natural abilities, physical features and general personality. Your self-image determines your belief system and your belief system determines the thoughts that drive your life. Your self-image is a result of the stories you accept within yourself unconsciously. If people have told you something negative and you accept it, this would drive your action until you unravel and change it. Daniel accepted he was good for nothing because his friends said so. He started changing his self-image when I showed him how his creator sees him. The Bible tells us clearly that we are fearfully and wonderfully made by God for dominion[4]. You might have been broken by circumstances, the words of family or friends. We must do unravel your belief system and ensure it aligns with you fulfilling your purpose. Let me share with you how belief systems can form and how strongly this can affect your life.

My dad had a jalopy which was very helpful in our early childhood years. The doors were difficult to close at a point. So, we banged the door with full force anytime we closed it. On travelling to Canada, I went out with a friend on a rented car. We enjoyed a beautiful ride that day on a virtually new car with very good doors too. After stepping down from the car, I unconsciously banged the door so hard that my friend shouted asking if I wanted to break the door. It dawned on me that my action that day was shaped by my experience from the past. A core part of me at that point believed that every car's door is bad, and this unconsciously determined my actions.

You may have failed at some point in life and this makes it difficult to see God's purpose in your life. However, your situations or outward things does not define who you are. Your being is different from your doing. You are a human being and not a human doing. You may have made a mistake at some point in life, you may have not achieved anything spectacular yet in life but one thing is clear, you are alive today because God has a purpose for your life.

In the next coaching session, I want you to be honest with the story of your self-image so you can get a right belief system to fulfil your purpose.

SELF-IMAGE MAP

A self-image map is a picture of your current self-image in different aspects of your life. It provides clarity on areas where you would need improvements so you can have a solid foundation for living a life of purpose.

On a range of 0 – 10, rate how much you feel each of these sentences describe you. 0 being wrong and 10 being exact.

1. A. I am intelligent

   B. I am not intelligent

2. A. I love the relationships in my life right now

B. I am not happy with my current relationships

3. A. I like the way I look

    B. I do not like the way I look

4. A. I am an extremely gifted individual

    B. I am not gifted at all

5. A. I have learnt a lot of lessons in life

    B. I have made too many mistakes in my life

6. A. If I don't get a job something is wrong with the system.

    B. If I don't get a job, something must be wrong with me.

7. A. I believe I can be great and add value to people's lives.

    B. I don't believe I can be anything great in life

8. A. If I encounter a challenge, I do everything to overcome it

    B. If I encounter a challenge, I quit trying.

9. A. I am not addicted to anything to make me feel happy.

B. I am addicted to something to make me feel happy.

10. A. I believe I can always do better than I do today.

B. I believe my peers are much better than me.

Sum your scores for all As and do so for all Bs. If you score above 70 in your As (and below 30 in Bs), you have a strong self-image that would give you confidence in achieving your life purpose. If you scored between 50 to 70 (and between 30 to 50 in Bs), you have a good self-image but with some room for improvements. Below 50 (and above 50 in Bs), requires more work to get a good self-image. The lessons shared next would help you build a positive self-image.

Your self-image depends on three components: your self-concept, self-worth and self-esteem.

Self-Concept: Your self-concept is who you believe you are based on your personal abilities. It defines who you believe you are ideally. For example, you could say I am an orator or a singer because of your speaking or singing abilities. In the self-image map, the rating on intelligence is an evaluation of your self-concept. If you rated yourself low in this, understand that intelligence is not necessarily about doing well in school examinations. It is the ability to acquire knowledge and apply them. This is an attribute that everyone excels at depending on the area of application. Not everyone is intelligent at everything.

It is what you believe you become.

The foundation for a right self-concept is understanding you are a winner. It is what you believe you become. Focus on the things you are good at and build a positive praise around that. You can also build a positive self-concept around who you are growing to become. For example, I am a leader developing millions around the world to live a life of purpose. My message may not have reached millions yet but this is who I am growing to be and I build my self-concept around that. A healthy self-concept helps you live with more confidence, keep growing and be purpose-driven.

Self-Worth: Your self-worth is the value you think you bring into people's lives. A positive self-worth means you believe you can impact the world. Like we shared already, if your self-concept is being an orator, a good self-worth means you believe you are a good orator. Everybody has something they are currently good or can be good at. If you scored yourself poorly in being an extremely gifted individual, you may want to take some time to think now about what you are good at or can be good at if you give some time to it. In Chapter two, you will see some examples of natural abilities that everyone has. Your self-worth depends on how well you know and love yourself. Without looking at outward things or things you cannot change, take some time to reflect on the intrinsic things you really love about yourself.

Self-Esteem: Your self-esteem is how you feel about your evaluation of yourself. A high self-esteem shows you feel good about yourself and your abilities. For examples a person with a high self-esteem does not only believe he is an orator but also feels good to be an orator. A low self-esteem usually stems from comparisons, lack of self-discipline and wrong affirmations. To build your self-esteem, you must stop comparing yourself with others. One person may be good at singing while another is a good orator. Be happy with who you are and choose rather to be better than who you were yesterday.

A low self-esteem can also result from a lack of self-discipline. Self-discipline helps you set your heart to do a thing and go ahead to do it. If you set to do a task and do not complete it, it affects your self-esteem subconsciously. To improve your self-discipline, start with tasks you can complete. Break down major projects into small tasks that can be easily completed. Avoid procrastination. Self-discipline is not built over night but over time, so be patient with yourself as you keep building your self-discipline and your self-esteem as a result.

The most powerful stories that affect your self-image, are the ones you tell yourself. Negative thoughts make you feel lowly of yourself. Instead of telling yourself, "I am good for nothing", you can say "I am the best and I add value to the people in my life". This would take a conscious effort of you giving yourself positive affirmations daily. Here are some affirmations to help you build a positive self-image.

Some positive affirmations:

"I am blessed and a blessing to my generation"

"I carry a purpose that must impact my world"

"I am wonderfully and fearfully made in God's image and likeness"

"I am beautiful in every way"

"I have a good heart that desires to bless people always"

"I am a person of value who desires knowledge and keeps growing"
"I am great, and God values me"
"I am unique, there's no other person like me on earth"
"I love myself in every way"
"I am the best"

An example of a positive self-image statement with a positive self-concept, self-esteem and self-worth would be:

> I am *talented*, I feel good about this and I believe my *talent* would bless millions around the world.

Spend time thinking and speaking these positive affirmations and any other ones you choose to yourself as much as possible.

The following activity would help you reflect on different aspects of your life. Take time to reflect deeply on these areas and write down how you make improvements or maintain your current level of satisfaction.

COACHING SESSION

On a scale of 1 to 10, 1 being the least and 10 being highest, rate how well you love your current activities in the following areas:

Career, School or Work

Relationships

Location

Personal development

In any of these areas where you have scored low, think about ways you can make improvements or discuss your options with your accountability partner.

Now that you have sorted the first thing of a positive self-image, let's look into how you can discover your goldmine.

CHAPTER THREE

DISCOVER YOUR GOLDMINE

"The two most important days in your life are the day you were born and the day you find out why"
-Mark Twain

Discovering your purpose as we see from the purpose triangle in chapter one is the foundation for its eventual fulfilment. Just the same way man's creations have clues about the reason for its creation, so God gives clues for us to know our purpose and walk in His clear plan for our lives. These clues manifest every day in the life of every man but for lack of knowledge, some ignore them. In this chapter, you would learn seven clues to guide you in discovering your life purpose.

In the purpose discovery circle in figure 2 below, you'll see an interaction between the God, clues, and time. In summary, to discover purpose, you must come to the author of life, God who created you, to find out the reason for which he gave you life. God can answer you through divine revelation or clues and when you don't get any of these, stay with God continuously to gain clarity. The revelation of purpose can be seen in the life of Joseph in the Bible. He got a revelation through a dream from God that he would be a leader. Even though he did not understand the details of the dream immediately, it was clear that God had a plan for his life. You'd also see the revelation aspect of purpose in the life of Jeremiah when God spoke expressly to him that He has ordained him to be a prophet to the nations.

Apart from the revelation aspect of purpose, there are *God clues* He uses to guide us on the path to purpose fulfillment. *God clues* either show up as your passion or natural abilities at childhood, if you don't get it then, it could show up again as a strong urge within your heart.

If you miss it again, they would show up as a challenge you have to overcome with your calling and once you breakthrough, you have your license to help others break through. God's clues are guides within your path to help you serve Him better and be a blessing to the world around you.

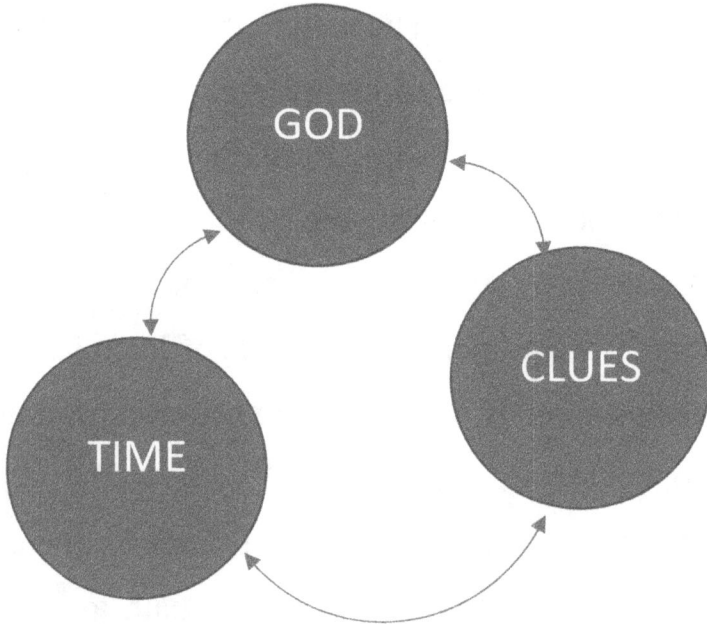

Fig. 2. Purpose Discovery Circle

The following are seven *God clues* to help you discover your goldmine.

It's in you

The first clue is the passion in your heart which usually shows up first at childhood. I had a childhood passion for writing lessons on life I believed would help people. This led me to write my first mini-book, I called *Facts of Life*. The book contained life principles I learnt from observing people. Well, I couldn't find this book after some time and I started focusing more on formal education. It was at the University that my passion to help people got ignited again and this was shown by my love for reading books. I read books that transformed my life but also with a passion to learn new things that would help me fulfill my life purpose of inspiring people.

Looking back now, if someone asked me then what my life purpose was, I may have answered cluelessly but with what I am doing today, I see my life purpose was always in my heart and manifested in my story from childhood.

> *If you must discover purpose, you must focus on who you are within and not what your outward situations define you to be.*

No one tells the sun when to shine, the purpose for which it was created is in it and so it shines according to its purpose. No one tells the trees when to grow, they grow in alignment with their purpose. This is how it is for man too, your purpose is in you, it would already manifest in some form of clues if you pay attention to the desires of your heart.

As I write this book, it's winter across Canada. During this very cold period, the trees adapt to the cold by shedding their leaves. As we get into spring when the weather becomes a bit warm, the trees begin to blossom again and bring forth their beautiful leaves. The cherry blossom is my favorite flower to view during this period. On reflection about these seasonal changes of trees, I started asking, who taught the trees how to adapt and how did the trees know what to do in any weather condition? I got a profound inspiration from this, that God put in all His creatures a mechanism to fulfil purpose irrespective of outward situations. If you must discover purpose, you must focus on who you are within and not what your outward situations define you to be.

The seed principle

I still think one of the most fascinating things that God made is the seed. With a seed, you have a tree and within that seed you have other seeds. When the seed finds the proper avenue for growth, it sprouts out everything within it. This is also true for purpose. Your purpose is like a seed within you which needs the right soil for you to find fulfillment. Your purpose is the seed and your vision is the tree. What you do with the seed today, determines the kind of tree you grow up to be tomorrow. Just as the tree does not come into a seed later so your purpose is not an afterthought from God. I always tell people, there is a seed of greatness in every man including you. Your greatness is in you. Your creative genius is in you. Your greatest resource to become all that God has called you to be is in you right now.

As we continue to drill further to discover your goldmine, the next clue helps you probe further into the desires of your heart to reveal the purpose in you.

What do you really want to do?

The question of what you love to do can be a very tricky one. Today people are in love with different things - games, drugs, sleep. It is not just anything you want to do but something that adds values to you and the life of others. What you really want to do to from your heart to add value to others is the clue of purpose discovery in your heart. Some people are frustrated by the struggles of children, women, poverty etc. The desires of your heart can either show in form of a passion or frustration. Mother Teresa felt a passion for the poor kids in India. Martin Luther King Jnr. felt frustrated at the treatment of blacks across America. You too can find your clue by paying attention to what makes your heart beat faster. What you really want to do from your heart many times would be things you are passionate about doing all day without asking for pay.

There is an experiment I want you to try now. Say these words out, "I would fulfill purpose". Shut your two ears with your index fingers and say same words would same tempo as the last time. Which is louder? Definitely the second time when your ears were shut. This is true because the sound from within you is louder when you shut your ears to distractions from the world. The answer to the question of purpose is usually clearer when we were kids. The period of childhood is the period of least resistance to dreams and aspirations. Our creativity is at the highest level and with careful observation it is easy to guess the purpose of a child at the early stages of development. Many people go on to fulfil their hopes and aspirations from childhood but some others drop them along the way due to a high tendency for conformation into the world's mold or the standards the world set for us.

To answer the question on what you really want to do, you should shut your ears to the world's distractions. What you really want to do is not anything the world has told you to be but what you are passionate or have a natural interest in.

What are your natural abilities?

God gives us natural abilities to help us fulfil his divine purpose for our lives. These are things that you can do effortlessly. People commend you for doing this excellently. Many of the stories you've read in this book are about people who connected with me through my writings. Writing is one of my natural abilities. I have committed to develop and use in helping people discover and fulfill God's purpose for their lives. It is important to know your natural abilities are a clue to your purpose but more importantly you should use them in fulfilling God's purpose for your life. The *law of use* for our natural abilities states that what you do not use you lose.

This was revealed in the story of the talents in the Bible. The Master shared talents amongst his three servants just before going on a long journey. On getting back, the servants with five and two talents had doubled their talents while the servant with one talent buried his talent with no multiplication. The Master called him wicked and gave his talent to the one with five[6]. The talent in this story is like our natural abilities. Do not bury your natural abilities by ignoring it's use.

Examples of natural abilities that are clues to your purpose:

Speaking

Writing

Drawing

Leadership

Analytical thinking

Creative thinking

Singing

Handcrafts

Teaching

Help

Empathy

Encourager

Giving

Intelligence

Programming   Event organization

Photography/Creative

Designing

To help you use your natural abilities to a more productive level that helps you maximize your potentials you must understand the concept of *flow*.

When I first started learning to play the piano, my fingers could not follow the keys properly. At some point I wondered if I could ever learn to play a complete scale on the piano successfully. This was also a similar experience when I tried learning to ride a bicycle. In both cases, I became good after repetitive trials. It became easy to play a scale on the piano and ride the bicycle almost unconsciously. I call this a state of flow very similar to a concept made popular by positive psychologist *Mihály Csíkszentmihályi*, in his book, *Finding flow.*

It is important to understand flow because you could quit on your natural ability if you do not use it to a state of flow. You may say you are not a good writer if you do not discipline yourself to write repetitively for some time till you get to flow. I believe flow is a characteristic of our brains. The brain is a muscle that forms patterns, also called neural pathways, according to its use. With repetitive use of your brain to develop a particular skill, the brain forms neural pathways that makes that skill flow unconsciously. The state of flow also increases your productivity as you use your natural abilities. To get to a state of flow, find out your natural abilities you may have left dormant for some time and find ways to use them repetitively with concentration and focus till you get to flow.

What are your current challenges?

Born without arms and limbs in 1982, Nick Vujicic contemplated suicide at age eight and attempted drowning in a bathtub at ten. He was frustrated at life and wondered why he was different from everyone else. His whole life changed one day when his mum showed him the newspaper story of someone else going through a similar struggle.

Realizing his struggles wasn't unique helped him embrace his challenges and see himself as an inspiration to many. He began to see himself differently once he understood that God had a plan for his life which includes overcoming his struggles to inspire others.

> *Your challenges can be used as a channel to changed lives rather than quench you.*

Today Nick is an inspiration to millions in the world through his non-profit organization, *Life without limbs.* He is an international best-selling Author and inspires people around the world with a message of hope and courage to overcome life's limitations. Like he said, "if I can encourage just one person in this life, my job is done".

Nick's story changed when he saw himself in the bigger picture of inspiring others through his story. From suicide to inspiration, discouragement to encouragement, a lack of hope to fullness of hope, all because he discovered God's plan for his life. This is the miracle of fulfilling purpose. It can totally transform your life and give you reasons to wake up to life with so much drive every day. Your current challenges can be a clue to the lives you are called to bless. Your challenges can be used as a channel to change lives rather than quench you.

Who do you attract?

The people you attract can also be a clue to your purpose. There are times when people can see in you what you do not see in yourself. When I started posting articles on Facebook, it was all in line with my purpose to inspire people, but it got more interesting when young people piled up on my inbox with different life questions. You may attract people with leadership questions if God's purpose for your life is to be a leader. You may attract people with questions about business if you are growing to be a business leader. Do not take the people you attract for granted or simply ignore the clues. It is an opportunity to review your life to build yourself up to walk in this purpose. Though it is not every time you attract people that it is necessarily a clue on your purpose. It must align with your inner drive within your heart. The people you attract should only be a confirmation because sometimes you may have to direct people to appropriate quarters to get help and not try to be everything to everybody.

Who is your role model?

Who you love is usually a clue of who you want to be. It reveals the inner yearnings of your heart. I loved inspirational speakers, like Mike Murdock, Myles Munroe, Pastor E. A. Adeboye, Bishop Oyedepo and many others. In retrospect I can say this was a clue of God's purpose within my heart. When you find your role models, you don't have to be exactly like them. You have your own uniqueness. Three questions to confirm if your role model truly reveals your purpose:

a) Are they adding value to lives?

b) Are they inspiring people with their story?

c) Are they morally upright?

If they pass these three tests in the affirmative, you can learn from them as mentors or role models to grow intentionally into purpose fulfilment.

What is your story?

Like road maps that guide you to an eventual destination, your story holds clues that guide you on the path to purpose fulfilment. Reviewing your life story reveals all the clues explained so far. Many times people are waiting for purpose to happen to them in future when purpose has already been with them. There's a friend, Donald, who was selected as a class leader at an early age even though he wasn't the best in class intellectually. He was selected as a hostel leader in boarding school and many other times he was selected as a leader in the most unlikely circumstances. If this person reviewed his story he would have known that his purpose was tied to him becoming a leader and also lead others but there is a tragic story about this I'd share in the next chapter on intentional growth.

Review your story to identify your natural abilities, your passion, who you attract and your role models. Taking time to reflect on your journey so far could produce the most significant moments that change the course of your life.

WHAT QUESTION SHOULD I ANSWER?

In the process of preparing this book, Josephine, a young girl of about eighteen years old, called me to explain how she was currently clueless about her life purpose. I was curious and asked why she thought so. She explained how people would always ask her the question: what do you love to do without being paid? And she had no answer to this.

I explained that everyone would have a different question to answer that unveils purpose and not necessarily what you love doing without being paid. Purpose is unveiled by a series of questions and not just one question. After asking a few questions and sharing my story, her childhood passion of encouraging people finally got unveiled. Your purpose is hidden in your heart and can be unveiled by divine revelation or a series of questions that review your life's story. It is also true that you may not possibly get a perfect clue on what your purpose is at some point in life but there would always be a clue to guide you in taking actions that guide you to the eventual fulfilment of your purpose.

Josephine has a clue that her goldmine is tied to encouraging people but eventually she may find herself encouraging people through music. She may find herself as a professional life coach helping people unveil life's answers within them and encourage them to live their best life. It is possible she even becomes an Attorney who stands for the weak and encourage them through tough legal battles.

You'd have a clue but give yourself time and flexibility to allow your journey reveal your purpose.

GIVE IT TIME

There was a man who sang so well that thousands admired him. He was gifted with a wonderful voice and wrote a lot of songs. With so many admirers, it didn't take too long before his name got to the king of his city.

The king had been going through an illness and one of his servants recommended this man's song to him. As predicted, his song healed the ailing king. His musical talent had taken him to stand before royalty. After a series of events, this man became the king of the city. His natural ability took him to a place of fulfilling purpose at a level that eventually paved the way for the ultimate fulfillment of seating on the throne as king. This is the story of David in the Bible[7]. Between discovery and fulfilment were several years of patience, building relationships and growth. One of David's natural ability was singing but as he grew towards fulfilment of purpose, he learnt writing, prophecy and most importantly leadership.

Depending on what clues get exposed to you at this level, you may need to give yourself time to gain clarity and keep growing before the ultimate fulfilment of your purpose. If what you have known is your purpose, is not what you see in your life currently, give yourself time and keep going back to God as your source to draw inspiration and revelation for a new level.

> *Your existence is evidence that this generation needs something your life contains.*
> *– Myles Munroe*

Give yourself time, everything would come together at the appropriate time. This is why the purpose discovery circle is a journey. In the Bible, Joseph got a clue at an early age, David got a clue at an early age, but Abraham got his at a later stage of his life. Life is like giving birth; an opossum has 12 to 13 days gestation period while an elephant has 640 to 660 days. However, the opossum lives for only 2 to 4 years while an elephant lives for 50 to 70 years. Ensure you are living a life of purpose and if you do not have clarity of purpose yet, give yourself time. Like Myles Munroe said, your existence is evidence that this generation needs something your life contains.

Discovery of purpose is not an end in itself, you must learn how to nurture what you carry and intentionally grow to be of impact to the world.

COACHING SESSION

1. Write down any significant event(s) that happened when you were a child that made you feel proud of yourself?

2. What natural abilities were you known for at childhood?
3. What did you love most about your childhood?
4. Write at least three role models you love their works?
5. What is common about these role models?
6. What question do people usually seek your help on?
7. What are the current challenges in your life that you feel a lot of people are also going through?
8. What would you love to do all day without asking for a pay?

   9. Review your answers from 1 to 8 above and write down any inspired thoughts you think about yourself.

CHAPTER FOUR

INTENTIONAL GROWTH

"Talent is a gift, but growth is a choice"

Donald was known for his leadership abilities at an early age. He was the first born in his family, he knew how to carry everyone along and people loved him. He was made the class prefect in all his classes and was also the head prefect at secondary school (high school). He also became the President of his student association at the University. Anyone who looked at his story was sure to know that his life purpose was tied to his excellent leadership abilities.

Today it doesn't seem like he is living that dream anymore. Life hassles, hustles and bustles have got him focusing on other things rather than living a life of purpose. Rising up the leadership ladder also attracted a lot of ladies to him and this caused some derailment. There are many things to point out why he may not be walking in his purpose today but one central point is clear, abuse is inevitable when purpose is unknown.

I don't want you to end up like that. This is why I urge you to take the coaching sessions and be deliberate in answering them. There is a path to follow on your road to fulfilling purpose, it is not enough to discover purpose, it is not enough to know your natural abilities or what you love to do. You must intentionally grow to become that person who fulfills purpose by a life of impact. Purpose in its raw state is a potential, what you do with it would determine whether you fulfill your purpose or not.

Discovery of purpose is like finding a natural resource under the earth. It is usually not useful at such crude state but the maximum potential is released after several stages of refinements. I was at a meeting one time discussing about a country in Africa. This country holds one of the world's largest reserves of gold worth trillions of dollars. However, these trillions have not been converted to a better quality of life for her citizens. This was a very clear example for me that, potential is not enough, converting it to fulfill purpose is more important. This is why refined gold is worth more than raw gold. Like John Maxwell said in his book, *Talent is never enough*, "The toughest thing about success is that you've got to keep on being a success. Talent is only a starting point in business. You've got to keep working that talent.". Talent is a gift, but growth is a choice. A deliberate choice to be your best and do your best.

So, what are the keys to refining your purpose for maximum impact?

Love is the foundation

The key to keep you growing to fulfill your purpose is having a heart of love. At a coaching session, my client had said, she found it difficult to speak in public during meetings where she knew she had so much to say but felt so little courage to say them. It was obvious she was prepared because she had enough knowledge to contribute. She got a profound insight when she realized that keeping valuable information to herself was selfishness. Love is the pipeline that allows our gifts flow from our hearts to bless others. When you grow in love, you would grow towards fulfilling purpose. Every other thing would be difficult to achieve if we do not fix the foundation of love. Purpose is not about money or fame or what you can get. Purpose is more about what you can give. There is a gift the world needs that only you can provide. Are you willing to use your gifts to bless lives? Are you willing to stand in the gap for the downtrodden? Are you willing to be a voice to the voiceless in the society? The answer to these questions is the measure of love your heart.

Knowledge

Knowledge is like fire in the furnace of gold refinement. Acquiring knowledge refines your gold to be more valuable and impactful. Receiving knowledge depends on your openness and willingness to ask questions. In this age of information overload, everyone is saying they read a book a month, a book a day with different new topics to learn every day and different skills to select from. Discovering your purpose helps you focus on the right knowledge that helps refine your purpose for fulfillment. When I discovered that I love to inspire people, I got more inspirational books to read in preparation. If you see yourself as leader, get books on leadership to prepare yourself.

> *The greatest secrets in the world are hidden in the hearts of men, some have been generous enough to put them in books.*

For every area of life where you need an improvement, read at least ten books (or one book ten times). I call this the *Rule of Ten*. This would make the knowledge stick with you till it becomes a habit. Knowledge alone does not transform but the inspired actions you take in form of habits are what really make the difference. Read at least ten good books on entrepreneurship if you want to imbibe the core principles that would make you an exceptional entrepreneur. Read biographies of your role models and mentors. Their success secrets are hidden in their stories. The greatest secrets in the world are hidden in the hearts of men, some have been generous enough to put them in books.

Be flexible but focused

A client, Jonathan, explained to me about how much he loved football, but his Father insisted he went to study Civil Engineering. At a young age of twenty, Jonathan was concerned about his footballing career if he waited till twenty-five before starting. He wasn't clear about his chances if he pursued a footballing career, but he was doing well above average in school. Without a clear opportunity to pursue a footballing career, he eventually chose to pursue an education to acquire knowledge that expands thinking but to keep building his footballing skills till an opportunity came up. He kept his focus on his growth but flexible about his opportunities to be more impactful in the society.

One of my favorite characters in the Bible, Joseph, had a natural ability to dream. As time went on, he grew to start interpreting dreams. He went through trials from the pit to prison till he eventually entered the center of his purpose of being a prime minister over Egypt. What if Joseph chose to remain a dreamer? What if he stopped at interpreting dreams? He would not be known today. Therefore, flexibility is important especially when it would increase your influence, impact and still be in line with your purpose. Gaining clarity is a journey that everyone goes through.

Getting started

One of the biggest hindrances to growth in fulfilling purpose is in getting started. So many of us are filled with ideas and all we would love to do. Sometimes the issue is not about purpose discovery but really getting started with that burning desire in your heart. I remember how I struggled with this on my first book, *Success Basics*. I knew I'd write books someday but just taking the time to finish it was difficult due to the mindset blocks that hinder many from getting started. There is always resistance in our minds that stops us from starting anything worthwhile. This is so because the brain is designed to maintain survival. It wants to keep you in your comfort zone to avoid potential disasters. It takes a conscious effort to go in the direction of your purpose, overcome your mind resistance and act. If you want to achieve anything meaningful in life, you must learn the art of execution.

You would not be getting inspiration from this book today if I didn't get started. You would have no phone today if Martin never got started. Think about people who have blessed you and what you would have missed if they never got started. Getting started is the seed for your intentional growth process. Starting creates an opportunity for you to learn and improve. No matter the great things you celebrate around you today, it all started from a small beginning. You must try if you want to grow. Even if you fail, you have not to make same mistake in your next try. He who fails to try tries to fail. He who never gets started never makes progress.

Skills

I didn't take out time to consider my natural abilities, my passion and to start building them as skills. I thought after discovery, fulfillment is automatic. I would write on Facebook, save some on my PC and hope that someday they would turn themselves into a book. Focusing so much on excelling in school, left out a part of me that was also important in fulfilling my divine purpose. Last year I chose to be more intentional about my writing, got a writing coach and got my first book published. Many gifts lie dormant when people don't invest in growing them into gifts. Invest in acquiring skills. Today we are breeding a generation that spends so much on what they do not like and seeking for freebies of what they love. Be willing to make the sacrifice whether financial or otherwise to invest in yourself. The best investment you can make is investment in your personal development and the best investment in your personal development is in acquiring skills that would be with you for as long as you live.

There is a principle of directed progression you must apply to make progress in life. The principle works for every aspect of life. The principle of directed progression helps you maximize your potential to be more impactful in the near future. Think about the kind of person you want to be and find out the skills you can develop to get there. Build up yourself and make progress in the direction of your end goal. If you feel called to sing songs, find out the skills you must develop to refine your gift. If you feel called to be a speaker, start developing your speaking skill by watching great speakers, attending seminars or taking courses. I remember listening to John Maxwell at a *Live to Lead seminar* share how he focused on developing his leadership and speaking skills. Today we see the result of that directed progression after many years as John is now an international leadership consultant, speaker and author of several books on leadership.

Mentors and Role Models

Mentors and role models are people who have gone ahead of you and learning from them can help you reach your full potential faster. Mentors are those you can ask questions closely while role models are those you can learn from at a distance. Congratulations if you can get access to a mentor who really cares about your speed and growth. Ask them questions that draw out wisdom from their experience. Who you give your "ear-time" could determine how far you go in life. Give your "ear-time" to the wise and you would become wise, give your "ear-time" to the foolish and they would drag you into failure. A wise man finds a wise mentor. Mentors are people who have gone ahead of you and are willing to show you the way. The learning curve to rise in life is really steep and could take you years but having a mentor is the shortest path to success because you would avoid the failures of your mentors.

It may not be easy to get mentors you know one-on-one but you can get role models who you glean from their wisdom through their books or online messages.

Even on social media, select the people you spend time with wisely, the rightful mentors would share inspiring messages to help improve your life while the time-wasters would share time wasting messages. If you have identified your role models, learn from their books, teachings and any lessons you can get from them. Attend events where you can meet these people and glean from their wealth of experience. Intentionality demands that you find these people through Google, social media and any way you can. You could spend years trying to figure out something your mentors or role model has already overcome and would most likely have shared lessons publicly. I started focusing on developing just two of my skills on writing and communication after listening to

John Maxwell share on how he focused on his communication and leadership skills in an intentional growth seminar. Before then I just read inspirational books without the bigger picture of developing a skill. Having the right mentors can be a very powerful asset on your journey to fulfilling purpose and so you need to understand how to attract them.

How to attract the right mentors

If you want to attract the right mentors, you must be clear about what you really need a mentor for. For example, if you are a baker, you'd have to check for mentors in the baking industry and not someone in the fashion industry. Clarity of purpose in seeking mentors also helps you identify the type of mentor with the requisite skill to train you. It is like going to a university, you don't select schools just because the names sound nice or others are going there. You select schools with your desired programme and course work.

In attracting mentors, you should understand their work and how it can add value to you. This would involve you asking questions in line with your interests to draw out lessons from their life's journey. It is wrong to have time with your mentors and keep asking irrelevant questions. Imagine discussing football matches all through an appointment with a doctor. If your mentor already has a business or a book, do not let them duplicate their efforts by stylishly trying to get that information for free. I have seen some people do this and it is very wrong. As much as you can, patronize their business and you'd get the opportunity to ask them for more. Patronizing them also show you value their business and you want to add value to them. A mentorship relationship should be of mutual benefit to both mentor and mentee.

It is also okay also if you have no mentors too. In this information age, there is enough information online for anyone to fly. It is wrong to keep wallowing in self-pity for lack of mentors especially as your purpose is unique to you. Remember you only need mentors for guidance and not permission. Your purpose in you is already enough permission for you to achieve greatness. Get the required knowledge for every phase of your life from role models and run with that.

Platforms

These are places you can take advantage of to start preparing for your ultimate fulfillment of purpose. My first speaking engagement was in church, it was also my first opportunity to lead a group of people as the church youth leader. After you discover your goldmine, you must intentionally find platforms to start deploring it to help people. Platforms can be online via social media, it could be in your local church like my case, a school environment or clubs. For example, *Toastmaster International* is a platform for speakers around a community to meet together and train in public speaking and leadership. Platforms like these help you practice in smaller groups to build confidence and grow to impact larger groups. Do not take platforms of growth and preparation lightly no matter how small. The small preparation platforms help you take advantage of opportunities from larger platforms.

The price of refinement

Focusing on this growth progress comes at a price of refinement. Gold is found in its raw state under the earth. To be useful, it goes through the fire of refinement to remove all impurities. The refined gold is much more expensive and useful than the raw gold. Your purpose and all you see yourself achieving on earth is usually discovered at a raw state, the growth process is what makes it more refined for maximum impact.

> *The price of refinement is what turns the potentials of your purpose into results that bless lives.*

The price of refinement could come in form of spending more time away from TV, social media and anything that adds no value to you. The price of refinement is what turns the potentials of your purpose into results that bless lives. One of the definitions of purpose is the responsibility you have to your generation. Until you see purpose as a responsibility you won't be willing to pay the price of refinement. The price of refinement could also be in form of money, you have to spend money in buying books, coaching sessions and certifications. Be willing to pay the price to get the prize of a fulfilled life. You may have been growing in an area of your life but still feel a vacuum within like there is much more that you can do. You would need to understand two aspects of purpose for you to grow in a balanced way that helps you find fulfilment in every area of your life.

THE DUALITY OF PURPOSE

In chapter one, we mentioned the general purpose for which God created man. To have dominion, be fruitful, multiply, replenish and subdue the earth. To fulfill this purpose, God makes men kings and priests[8]. A king is someone who has dominion over a domain while a priest is someone who serves a group of people. God makes men kings so they can have dominion in the place of their purpose and priests so they can serve others freely in honor of God. This is the duality of purpose - to dominate as a king and serve as a priest. Kingship positions you to receive and priesthood positions you to give. Understanding the duality of purpose helps you live life as a channel and not a container. If you only focus on kingship, you would be selfish as you keep receiving but never give while focusing on your priesthood only would drain you as you keep giving and never receiving. There is no limit to what a channel can receive because it keeps giving and receiving but a container has limited capacity. Your priesthood is usually from a place of your passion; things you love to do without asking for a pay. People who focus on their priesthood find it difficult to ask for money for offering services. On the other hand, people who focus on kingship ask for money for everything. Your priesthood is your service to humanity, your community, your church while your kingship is the value you bring to the world, something you know the world needs and are willing to pay you for. For example, I teach in church virtually every Sunday, I give free articles on Facebook, and also give short counselling sessions to people for free when I have the time. These are some of the things I do as my priesthood in service to humanity. For my kingship, I am an expert data scientist, life coach, writer and online publishing consultant. My intelligence and analytical thinking ability help me dominate as a king and serve as a priest. If you've been serving as a priest or king only, this would be a good time to start looking at opportunities where you could serve or areas where you could create a business around to receive. The duality of purpose image below can help you in reflection.

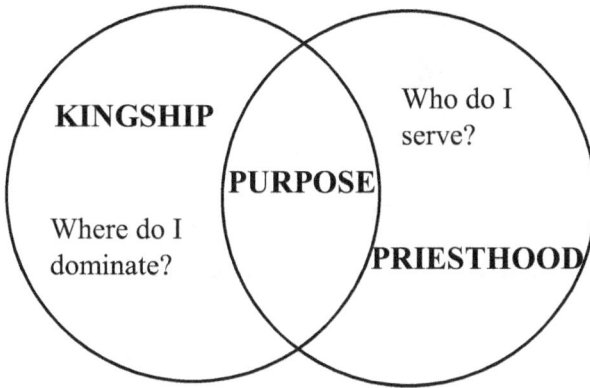

Fig. 3 The duality of purpose.

COACHING SESSION

1. Do you see yourself as someone who loves others or more concerned about yourself?

2. What knowledge (books, certifications, seminars) are you currently acquiring in line with your purpose?

3. What skill do you think you can develop to help fulfill your purpose?

4. In what areas of your life can you be more flexible in trying out new things?

5. a. What projects, tasks or plans have you been procrastinating to start someday?

b. Put a timeline to act in (5a) above.

6. a. Who are your mentors or role models?

b. Which of them can you schedule a meeting for a discussion on purpose?

7. What platforms can you use to start fulfilling purpose?

8. To identify your priesthood, ask yourself these questions:

a) What is my passion that I'm willing to do without a pay?

b) What areas can I serve in my community?

9. To identify your kingship, ask yourself these questions:

a) What am I good at that people are willing to pay for?

b) What skills can I learn that would impact the world?

When you start following the path for intentional growth towards your purpose, there are challenges that come along the way and you must understand how to overcome them, so you can keep growing.

CHAPTER FIVE

OVERCOMING CHALLENGES

"Let the rains fall,

Let the snow fall

Let the sun shine

Or the darkness come

I owe my generation my light

It is a debt I must pay

Come what may"

At an early age, I observed how I was always scared to speak in public. There were moments in a group discussion where I'd have something important to say but allowed it burn inside me until I lose concentration all through the meeting. The first time I remember standing in front of a crowd was in a children's programme in church. The children's coordinator had asked each child to make a presentation, so I accepted to make a Bible recitation. I practiced with several verses from the book of proverbs. I got on stage and spoke only the few I could muster courage to recite. I don't remember speaking in public after that until I was called to be an MC for an event in church. With proper preparation with inspirational stories, I got on stage with so much confidence and gave a superb performance. It was then I knew public speaking was part of my purpose and proper preparation was important to dispel fear.

There are different challenges that could stop people from fulfilling their purpose. What if I allowed fear keep me from public speaking? Of course, I won't be maximizing my potentials today.

Just like anything worthwhile in life, there would be challenges when you discover your purpose and have made up your mind to start growing. In this chapter you learn how to overcome the commonest challenges to fulfilling purpose.

Overcoming fear

I was successful on my first try to ride a bicycle and got enough confidence to ride on a major street in my neighborhood. Something kept recurring though. Any time a vehicle came in the opposite direction, I would lose my balance with shaky hands and fall off the way.

I wasn't sure why I kept falling off even though I was already good at riding. A time came when I heard in my heart to stay firm, summon courage and have no fear of any incoming vehicle. To my utmost surprise, I rode across peacefully as several vehicles passed me by. It occurred to me at that point that fear was behind my loss of balance.

Fear is the most dangerous emotion that limits men. Zig Ziglar defined fear as *False Evidence Appearing Real.* Even though the vehicles were on the other lane of the street, fear gave a false evidence like they were coming directly at me. Fear can make you lose balance and do many unlikely things. Fear can make you lose confidence in your abilities. It makes you believe all the "what ifs", magnifies your failures and trivialize your successes.

The only way to overcome fear is by intentionally building your confidence to go against it. You must understand the language of fear so that you can reject it and choose the language of faith. When fear says: *"What if you fail?"*, Choose faith and say: *"I can succeed, I will succeed, and I will make it."* When fear says: *"You are a failure,"* Choose faith and say: *"I may have failed but I am not a failure. I have several successes. I am made for success and significance."*

Focusing on problems magnifies your fears but focusing on possibilities magnifies your faith. Don't allow fear to limit you from achieving your purpose. Start that new thing you have had in your heart for long. Choose faith over fear every day. In the coaching session at the end of this chapter, you would coach yourself to replace your fears with faith.

Fear is not always limiting except when it is excessive and keeps us from walking in purpose. Think of one moment you were young and really afraid to act. For me it would be crossing the major road or climbing the stairs. The thought scared me and I always needed an adult to help me through. Today, I am not scared of crossing any road or climbing any stairs. Did the roads or stairs change? No! The fear was an illusion in mind and this was positive because I could possibly have caused some damage if I did it myself. I am more prepared now to take a calculated action on faith to cross any road or climb any stairs. If you have overcome the fears of your childhood, is it possible the fears you have now is only a lack of adequate knowledge or preparation? If you are confident you have the prerequisite knowledge to start walking in your purpose, you should act now. You should take more time to prepare if your fear is an indication of a lack of preparation.

Overcoming past failures

Failure is part of the learning process to help you grow in fulfilling your purpose. Failure is not final. Anyone who has never failed has never tried anything new. Do not be discouraged when you fail but rather be thankful you have learnt lessons that would make you much better positioned for a life of purpose. Many times, people quit and never try again because of a past failure. You must have a never-give-up mindset if you want to fulfil purpose.

> *You can either allow failure to be an extinguisher of your purpose or a propeller into greater heights.*

The first time I failed in my academic pursuit was in my second year. You know failure can be very shocking for the first time. Instead of getting discouraged, it made me resolve with all my heart to get a first class. You can either allow failure to be an extinguisher of your purpose or a propeller into greater heights. What you do with failure is up to you.

If you've had a rough past due to several failures, you must understand like the Bible says that all things work together for good. When there is life there is hope. It is never too late to start living a life that leads to success again. A rough past can be seen as a lesson rather than a death sentence. If you can breathe, then you have enough strength within you to start changing your life. Everyone would have challenges at some point in life but how you react to it is what makes the difference between champions and quitters. Like I wrote in my book, *Success Basics*, "Cowards die many times but the valiant only die once". Do not put a full stop in your life where God only placed a comma. On the other side of your challenges are many people waiting to also be free. You can rise from a rough past and become a light that everyone looks up to when they hear how you turned that test to a testimony.

My friends are already making progress

A major enemy of purpose is the desire to be like everyone else. You could drown in the sea of sameness when you don't stand out with the seed of your uniqueness. You must be focused on where you are going to and what it takes to get there. Individual timings for impact are different. Like I mentioned in the *principle of gestation,* the gestation period for your purpose could be very different from that of your friends.

I know this challenge is even more serious today because of social media. People are comparing their real lives with the fake lives of others on the internet. People are only putting make-believe lives on social media to generate traffic and possibly generate sales. You should focus on building your real life with the potential for a more lasting impact rather than a fictitious make-believe life. When all is said and done, it is the life you build that would count rather than the life you make others believe you have.

When your friends are making progress, be happy for them and avoid envy. If the lion had envy, it would not be the king of the jungle. The lion is not the fastest animal, it is not the biggest animal, and neither is it the tallest animal, yet it is the king of the jungle. Focus on your lane and avoid comparisons. You are the king of your own jungle. You are the best, congratulate others when it's their turn to shine, your turn would also come. When the temptation to envy comes, remove it from your heart and declare to yourself, *'I was made in the image and likeness of God and not the image of any man'*.

Overcoming bad habits
Everything you would read in this book is to help you discover your purpose and understand how to fulfill it so

you can develop the habits for a purpose driven life. The challenge for many is to assume the knowledge would be enough but what really changes your life are the habits you acquire as a result of this right knowledge. Don't stop at acquiring the knowledge shared herein; also mind your habits.

> *Who we become is not merely about what we know but what we do with what we know makes the difference.*

Have you ever been in a situation where you knew what to do but then you don't do it? For example, you know you should study more than watching irrelevant TV programmes but then when an interesting programme comes on, you find yourself glued to your TV for hours non-stop. I had an interesting scenario like this, I knew for some time that I should brush my teeth in the morning before having my bath. Unknown to me, it had become a habit to have my bath before brushing my teeth. Several times, I had my bath before recalling I needed to brush my teeth. Don't laugh at me. I probably picked up this habit in boarding school where we had little or no drinking water but some dirty stream water to have our baths. When I eventually identified this habit, it took a conscious effort to change this and to keep choosing the right habit until it became an unconscious habit too.

This was a striking lesson that who we become is not merely about what we know but what we do with what we know makes the difference. Developing purpose driven habits takes a conscious effort. A purpose driven individual is conscious about the use of time in fulfilling purpose. Your time usage is the best way to evaluate your desire to fulfill purpose like you'd see in the coaching session.

To quit or not

Mikaela had a childhood passion for helping the downtrodden. She'd see sick and homeless people along the way and feel strongly drawn to help them. She felt in her heart to study nursing to help sick people and find opportunities to counsel the downtrodden. Even though she had told her parents about this, they had other plans for her. Her father is an engineer and wanted Mikaela to take after him as an aeronautic engineer. He could not imagine his daughter becoming a nurse.

Mikaela's respect for her parents made her apply to be an aeronautic engineer at the University and eventually got admitted. It didn't take too long into her programme before she started struggling. Respect for her father could make her start, but it didn't give her enough fuel to get to the finish line. Waking up daily to think she had to get to the finish line as an Aeronautic engineer was simply a night mare.

There are many variants of Mikaela's story out there today. Some are working at nine-to-five jobs they do not love. Some are in a location only due to a search for greener pastures. Some are in relationships not in alignment with their purpose. Some are living a life of drug addiction and secretly cry at night and wish that life could be better. If any of these describes you, obviously the next question would be whether to quit or continue.

The answer to this question can be very contextual and needs some level of coaching to unravel the right answer for each situation. In general, there are many situations you could interpret wrongly if you see purpose as a destination rather than a journey. There are times when your current level may not be your purpose but it holds the lessons to prepare you for fulfilling your purpose.

This can be seen in the life of Joseph. Potiphar's house was not his purpose but it held a lesson in administration as Potiphar gave him charge over everything in his home except his wife[9]. This training was definitely needed in fulfilling his purpose as a leader over Egypt. The prison was also not his purpose but he learnt leadership over prisoners which prepared him with leadership skills to lead Egypt. Your course may not be in line with your natural abilities but it could be an opportunity for you to learn discipline, hardwork and perseverance which would definitely be valuable for fulfilling your purpose.

For relationships, there are four kinds of people we would meet in life. People who add to you, multiply you, subtract from you or divide you. You should quit relationships in the last two groups but for marriage I'd recommend seeing a marriage counsellor or discuss with your partner more openly about pursuing a life of purpose together.

There are also times when you could give excuses and blame others when you do not see your purpose as your responsibility to your generation. Quitting school would not cure laziness, quitting a relationship would not cure anger, quitting your job would not cure a lack of work ethic. Do not be quick to quit when you need to develop the right attitude. You should pay attention to your character if you must fulfill purpose. You could quit on your outward situation but your character is an inward thing that would follow you anywhere you go.

The challenge of the multi-talented

Several years ago, I got my first desktop computer. I was excited to start learning web design, programming and many other exciting things. I started learning Dream Weaver, used for web designing. It didn't take too long before I left it and moved on to learn something else. Visual Basic programming was the only programming language I remember mastering during my undergraduate studies. At the same time, I started learning Java but couldn't go far with this either.

Since then, I have tried learning many things at the same time. At a time, I even attended a seminar on phone repairs. The only thing I can remember from that day is the color of the working equipment. I also remember learning forex trading but never implemented a trade. I could go on and on to tell you many things I have learnt at the same time but never implemented or mastered. I believe this was part of my growth phase in exploring several idea but many multi-talented never develop the discipline and focus to exploit a specific area of growth. This challenge can be overcome by proper time management and focusing on mastery. Depending on how much time you have, you can develop one or two skills at a time but focus on mastery. Develop to the extent you can be of service to people as a king and a priest. You know you have gained mastery when you start getting the results for which you developed that talent in the first place.

Many times, it is not because you do not have enough knowledge but because you are trying on too many things at a time. Choose rather to focus on one or two, at most three, master these before moving on to the next if necessary.

Overcoming the plateau of enthusiasm

Have you ever had that feeling when you get the idea to start a project and you get all pumped up, excited and feel so enthusiastic like the world is under your feet already but when you get started, you find out there were many i's not dotted and t's not crossed? You must have had some enthusiasm to start new projects in pursuit of purpose as you read through this book. Enthusiasm is a high level of excitement due to the anticipation of joy at the completion of a project. This happens when you start a new course you love, a new project, business, relationships etc. Enthusiasm is good because it gives us the drive to start these exciting endeavors. The challenge comes when enthusiasm gets to its peak and begins to plateau. This plateau usually comes possibly at the first challenge or boredom from repetitive activities. Some misinterpret this as signals for quitting or a lack of passion when it could have been turned into a signal for innovativeness and the application of a conscious effort to keep pushing. Do not bury your ideas under the plateau of enthusiasm.

Enthusiasm without knowledge is no good[10], acquire the requisite knowledge and plan properly before taking on that assignment. It is important to write down your goals and plan before you go into a new endeavor with only enthusiasm. Your written plan and adequate preparation would help you keep track if you get a plateau of enthusiasm.

What if no one believes in me?

The people of Israel were challenged at a time by a giant, Goliath[11]. No one could confront him as he looked far bigger than them and possibly had more experience at war than any of the Israelite army. Then came the young man, David, who decided to challenge Goliath. No one supported him, his brothers were angry at him for taking up the challenge. The king, Saul, recommended he puts on the army regalia to confront Goliath. Despite the contradictions, David, had confidence in God that he was able to defeat Goliath. He knew from his past dealing with God that he was well able to defeat Goliath. David went ahead to defeat Goliath with a totally unique technique. The people started singing his praise after he defeated Goliath[12].

This is also true in life, you do not need permission from any man except God to walk in the fulfilment of your purpose. What God reveals to you is more important than what anyone would say to stop you. David believed in himself. The most important person who must believe in your purpose is you. Do not be discouraged when no one believes in you. The most important question to answer is: do you believe in your purpose? The level of your belief in you would determine the possibility of fulfillment of your purpose.

Step out in your uniqueness like David. Many times, people would want you to fit into the world's mold. Dare to take a chance on your dreams. The people who do not believe in you today would soon come to your rising. Your best answer when people do not believe in you is to take actions to prove your purpose with results.

In the following coaching session, take out time to reflect on challenges you need to overcome on your journey to fulfilling purpose.

COACHING SESSION

1. a) Do you remember the last time you failed at something?

b) What lessons did you learn?

2. a) List every day of the week and mention what you spend each hour doing majorly.

b) What do you need to spend more time on and what do you need to spend less time on?

3 a) What are your fears about getting a job, relationships, starting a business, new project?

b) Which of these fears are real? The future ones are unreal, the past ones are not necessarily going to repeat. In the present you can evaluate your fears and go against them. Let faith lead you and not fear.

c) Write beside each fear, what you'd do if you had no fear.

4. In what areas do you need to believe more in yourself and act?

CHAPTER SIX

PUTTING IT ALL TOGETHER

"The only true success in life is fulfilling your life's purpose"

What legacy would you live for? This is a very important question that people never ask till death stares them in the face. Your purpose is the legacy your life would leave behind on earth. What would you want to be remembered for? People are not celebrated for what they destroyed but for what they helped build. Fulfilling purpose means focusing on the value you want your life to add in the end and living in alignment with that today. In this chapter, we put everything together to help you start taking actions in alignment with your purpose. The following are some examples of people who lived a life of purpose.

Martin Luther King Jnr.

Everyone who hears the name Martin Luther King Jnr. connects it to the liberation of blacks across America. King was frustrated at the segregation between whites and blacks. As a kid, he could not play with his friends who were whites. This racial humiliation stirred resentments in his heart but rather than fight this problem with hate, he chose to be a light to build a new society entrenched in love, equity and justice to all men irrespective of color differences. King was quick to connect this desire in his heart with his natural ability to speak eloquently. He discovered this gift as part of the debate team at Booker T. Washington high school. As he campaigned for a better society with so much passion and vigor, he lived for it and eventually died for it. He is an example in our generation of a man who fulfilled purpose and lived for a legacy doing what he believed in.

Jesus Christ

The story of a life of purpose is incomplete without the story of our LORD Jesus Christ. The perfect example of what it means to fulfil purpose. Jesus came with a clear mandate in mind. To deliver the oppress and reconcile man back to God. He mentioned his life purpose statement clearly in Luke 4:18-19.

> *"The Spirit of the Lord is on me,*
> *because he has anointed me*
> *to proclaim good news to the poor.*
> *He has sent me to proclaim freedom for the prisoners*
> *and recovery of sight for the blind,*
> *to set the oppressed free,*
> *to proclaim the year of the Lord's favor."*
> *– Luke 4:18-19*

His purpose was clear and He went through a process of growth for its fulfilment. His life was not about the longevity of years but the significance of impact. Over two thousand years after his death and resurrection, He is still the most popular person in world history. His life teaches us what it means to fulfill purpose, to do all that God has called you to do.

A picture of fulfillment

Recently on a taxi ride to church, I had a very emotional conversation with my cab driver. He is an elderly man possibly in his 60s. As we drove down talking about life in generally, he suddenly broke down almost driven to tears. He explained how he had so much money in the past and enjoyed the supposedly good life. He made a lot of money as a hedge fund manager, but he lost it all to a carefree life. His complaint that day was not about getting back all the money and it wasn't about getting back that good life. He said, "I just need peace. I just need peace, I feel so afraid of my next line of action". Thank God I could pray with him and he got inspired with an idea on the next steps to take.

The carefree life did not give him peace. All the money he had did not give him peace and fulfilment. As you go through life, it is important to have a big picture in mind. A big picture defines what the ultimate fulfilment for your life would look like. Would fulfilment be about the number of cars you acquired or the number of lives you blessed? Success without fulfilment is the ultimate failure and only in living in alignment with your purpose would you ever find fulfilment.

Living with a sense of purpose

I understand we have been talking more about the bigger picture of what your life would count for. Purpose is not only in the bigger picture though, it is a lifestyle lived every day. Purpose is fulfilled in every area of our lives when we live with a sense of purpose every day. As a Mother for example, living with a sense of purpose guides you in training your children to be people of value. A Father who lives with a sense of purpose understands his responsibility to care for his family. An employee who lives with a sense of purpose makes his highest contribution to the success of their employer. Living with this sense of purpose in every area of your life is what eventually adds up to a life of purpose.

You can now create a life purpose statement that puts together all you've read in this book.

Your life purpose statement

A life purpose statement is a clear representation of what you want to live for. It helps you put all your natural abilities and passion into a simple statement easy to remember to keep you always in alignment with your life purpose. As you grow and gain more clarity into your life purpose, it is possible for this statement to change over time. What should stay the same is the central theme for your life purpose. Your central theme can be the general purpose for which God made man, to glorify God in all you do.

A simple format you can use to craft your statement is:

- I have *natural abilities and skills* to help people in my *passion area.*
- I help people in my *passion area* with my *natural abilities and skills.*

Examples of life purpose statements:

- *"I am an intelligent writer and inspirational speaker to help people discover and fulfil God's purpose for their lives."*
- *"I help the downtrodden and neglected in the society to start life again with my empathetic heart and ability to attract help from rightful sources."*
- *"I want to use my skill in programming to develop a mobile app for people struggling in their mental health to find help easily and sound medical advice."*
- *"I help children with disabilities live a hopeful life with the lessons I've learnt from living above disabilities"*
- *"I help couples have heaven on earth marriages with the lessons I've learnt from having a happy home"*
- *"I use my intelligence and programming skills to help my company be the best in the market. I am a loving Dad to my children, so they can grow up to*

be blessings to their generation. I am a loving husband to my wife and I help her fulfill God's purpose for her life"

Lastly, I want you to know that it is possible to have a great purpose in life and yet not fulfill it. It is possible to have so many ideas of impact and yet never impact any life with these. It is possible to wait for someday to act and yet that day never comes. All this is possible but this is not the story I want for you. I have written this book to inspire you to act and keep shining your light to make the world better than you met it. This is your responsibility to your generation. Make us proud!

COACHING SESSION

1. What legacy would you love to live for?

2. Combine your natural abilities and passion to define your life purpose statement.

REFERENCES

1. Case A, Deaton A. Mortality and morbidity in the 21st century. *Brook Pap Econ Act* 2017.

2. Genesis 1:27

3. Ecclesiastes 1

4. Genesis 1:28

5. Hebrews 11:24-25

6. Genesis 12:4

7. 1 Samuel 16 – 2 Samuel 24

8. Revelations 5:12

9. Genesis 39:5

10. Proverbs 19:2

11. 1 Samuel 17

12. 1 Samuel 18:6-7

www.ingramcontent.com/pod-product-compliance
Lightning Source LLC
Chambersburg PA
CBHW020552030426

42337CB00013B/1062